D0416870

VOICE UNACCOMPANIED

VOICE UNACCOMPANIED

Poems

PHILIP MARTIN

AUSTRALIAN NATIONAL UNIVERSITY PRESS

CANBERRA 1970

Registered at the General Post Office,
Sydney, for transmission by post as a book.
National Library of Australia card no. and
ISBN 0 7081 0454 1
Library of Congress Catalog card
no. 79-120597

To my family and my friends

What is the thing which men will not surrender?
It is what they have never had, I think,
Or missed in its true season.

Richard Wilbur

ACKNOWLEDGMENTS

Some of these poems have appeared
in *The Age*, *The Australian*, *Compass*
(Melbourne University), *Meanjin
Quarterly*, *Melbourne University
Magazine*, *Orpheus* (Monash
University), *Paston's Melbourne
Quarterly*, *Poetry Australia*, *Quadrant*,
Twentieth Century (Melbourne), and
in the anthologies *Australian Poetry*
and *Poetry in Australia, Vol. II:
Modern Australian Verse*. Some have
also been broadcast by the A.B.C.
The lines from Richard Wilbur's
poem 'Running' appear in his
volume *Walking to Sleep* (Harcourt,
Brace and World) and are quoted by
permission of the author. In each case
my grateful acknowledgments
are due.

CONTENTS

CONTENTS

VOICE UNACCOMPANIED

THE FIRST OF AUTUMN

So freshly now the leaves begin their falling
It might be the first autumn of the earth,
The ritual waking at its origins:
These trees embraced by the matronal river
In silence but for a trout's leap, a bird calling
Lightly, briefly, to nothing, across pure space,
Perform their part in time with a live stillness;
I drift through the first autumn this clear morning
Before the gardeners put their rakes to use
And children or a girl in trouble find
Enough leaves to shush before their feet:
Autumn will deepen soon enough, but now
The spirit lifts as once when innocence
Was a word that breath and tongue had not forgotten.
As, in one sense or many, all must fall,
Grant us the gift of mime: to watch, go out
Into these trunks and branches to the tips
And know what they know, be such leaves in falling.

AGAIN AND STILL

Again and still I find you:
You are at the roots of my life,
Growing where I am growing.

And will be. Joyful sorrowing,
I say yes to this, and yes:
You are mine and never mine.

My face carries your light
(For this man entering the room
To see, if he should care to).

Flame stirring in coals,
You are a moving stillness;
To whom I move in stillness.

THIS CHILD

This child of dream, disturbance of your body
Feared even though desired, stirs now in me:
Comes through the shut gates, but like all children,
To be fed at your known breasts, though in a world
Ruled by ours a world of speculation.

Cradled there unbegotten, by your palpable fingers
Dressed and undressed, bathed, dosed in sickness;
Rebuked when necessary, calmed in nightmare;
Growing to learn your dignity in resource
From the first flow of blood; gaining your balance
Between the calm and wild: wine in a glass
Set dancing by deft hands yet never spilled.

So to unfold, set out on her own world.
She is herself and not to be predicted,
But takes, in dream, grey eyes from your grey eyes,
Her mouth from yours, soft within definition;
Wearing my dark hair as it may please her,
And please a man, in the fashion of a day
Not you, nor I, nor they may once experience.

The midnight swirls, I cannot see her clearly,
Moving as she does in dream, in the far corners
Of a room waiting for unbreaking daylight.
Yet, love, although the seed was lost, her shape
Cut upon darkness we conceived her truly.

MYTHS

1. ORPHEUS, PERSEPHONE

In a blank place, where boughs hang without wind,
Between the world and underworld he idles,
His lyre untouched, the void world left behind,
Ahead the creature of his search forgotten.
What messenger with wings about his ankles
Speeds to remind him?

She who gathering flowers was torn from earth
Is freed from the dark urn: earth expects her,
And till she comes it cannot flower again.
But still she loiters among sunless meadows,
Trees that will never flower, and hears no impulse;
Her skirts are empty.

2. ANOTHER PART OF HADES

But worse than Tantalus.
That fruit was shadow fruit whisked into air
When his hand reached towards it.

Here the fruit is real,
The love held out as warm as apricots.
The hand, unstirring,

The hand, only, is shadow.

HEAD OF A GIRL

On Vermeer's painting
of a young girl in a
turban

You turn your head to speak: lips just apart
And calm eyes pausing where the unseen brush
Moves, fixing your pose. A certain truth,
And yet no grain and roughness of the fact.
Visible blemish none, none from within,
No shadow growing with your womanhood:
Frigidity or tantrum or unrest
Such as no man could help, a need perhaps
Fretting content and strength from someone's life.
Peace, now, on all of this: here you are still,
Each looks on you as though a finite God,
Caught in the strict necessities of time,
Should judge you wholly on this simple gaze
And in swift acquiescence call you home.

FARMER'S SONG

for Chris

Which is the scarecrow here? We have it hard,
Waving our arms about by dusk and day
While the Lord holds in his wisdom and regard
The sweet birds that peck my crops away.

It's the same end to every fruitful season:
Ears hollow, cherry-boughs raw-pipped.
Yet a voice murmurs against fruitless reason,
Be glad, accept. And oddly, I accept.

FOR THE TOMB OF HERRICK

Here in silence
The summer gone
Herrick lies;
Who yet sings on.
But had he paused
Longer to pray
He might have found
No word to say
Of wanton eyes
And loosening hair;
And clearer seen
Earth's sentence there.
Who knows but God?
May God who knows
The delicate things
His spirit chose
Out of delight
As his bequest,
And knows their grace,
Draw him to rest.

SOUND AND SHELL

AN ENGLISH MARTYR

Tower of London, 1535

Now winter and all death are past.
Returning birds, returning leaves
And sun returning: can it be
That any heart this morning grieves?

And surely none grieves less than mine
Which in an hour shall beat no more.
O men unborn who, looking back,
Count me dishonoured and most poor,

I need no tears: I leave behind
All change of seasons and of men,
The pomp and treachery of kings,
Corruption, agony and sin.

The fine and running sand that marks
The hour sifts down within the glass.
A little longer and it's spent:
So lightly may this spirit pass.

And warmth of sunlight falling still
Upon this hewn, this bitter stone,
I take as greeting from my Lord
And rise up joyful to be gone.

YOUNG MAN'S SONG

The wind under the moon,
The moon in a rippled sky,
Clouds in the deep south-east
Towering and solitary,

And the clear heart awake,
Trembling to the least
To-and-fro of the air;
After the cold months' waste

Spring treads the night,
A presence in wind and moon;
The year's bride comes, but you—
When will you come, unknown

Soul and flesh to be loved
By this yet single heart?
Expectant and alone
But steadied with hope I wait

For the eventual wind
To carry you to me,
And the moon seems uplifted
To light your infinite way.

THE SHELL

I am a shell
That she, superbly heedless, has cast up
On a beach where listeners' footsteps never come.

And I, her shell,
That no one puts to his ear to learn her sound,
Am filled with the wash and pulse of driven water,
The restless to-and-fro, the unceasing over-
And-over of her heart.

My purpose and my glory to resound
Her secret sea, in secret.

SONG

for Georgina

Was it a word, or a look,
Or some brief carelessness,
Or self intruding just a step too far
Into the no-man's land where all love grows?
I cannot guess what light wind shook
The morning pearl from the spray,
What frost or burning air
Withered the blossom while I looked away.

IN THE LONG VACATION

for Fiona Bury

The Ormond clock has spoken
Ten words into the night,
Footsteps have all receded,
The moving clouds are bright
Between the towers and the moon;
I tread these flags alone.

Summer has brought its silence
Upon this dancing-place
You knew, of steps and voices:
I walk a wilderness,
And the moon rides from the east
Laying the faint stars waste.

And I must send you these
Mute words, for place and time
Bid them arise and seek you
As a recurring dream
Calls to the heart all day
Though sleep has fallen away.

The silence rings with parting,
Present and still to be;
The dancing will end, and Orpheus
Lose Eurydice:
A fading shape of white
She moves to the dense night.

And here between bell and bell
I stand, who may not go
Where the proud horse will take you
And the summoning winds blow.
The pattern breaks: I stay,
And you are riding away.

Melbourne University, 1956

IN MARCH

Be mute, this autumn, gather in the world,
And let the soft-trilled cricket speak for you
From the warm grass or through the wakeful night
Among late-fallen leaves and the smell of dew.
Be still, the season's voices call like sleep
And yet sing you to your waking: so
After long winter people in cold lands catch
The soft clear cry of water under the snow.

FOR A GATHERING OF POETS

The dying year goes out in rain and cold,
Shadow of winter overhangs the time,
And in this death men find their deaths foretold.

A violent end: the passing-bell is tolled
For a poet killed on the roads, who had some fame;
The dying year goes out in rain and cold.

May we not die before we've time to mould
Some perfect thing in grave and intricate rhyme,
Where men may find the peace of death foretold.

And may our faltering resolution hold
Though a poet die still young and the wind scream;
The dying year goes out in rain and cold.

May our achievement comfort us when old,
And hearten those who come the way we came,
That they may find in us their deaths foretold.

O Child, we bring You incense, myrrh and gold,
Dwell in our storm, O Peace and living Flame;
The dying year goes out in rain and cold,
And in this death men find their deaths foretold.

New Year's Eve, 1955

THE WINTER OF GERRIT ACHTERBERG

*Gerrit Achterberg (1905-62), the
Dutch poet who during a period of
insanity killed a woman he had
known.*

Where shall I find your beating heart?
Not even in a winter dream,
For the dead there have turned to stone;
And what grave magic can impart
Warmth to the grey curve of a cheek
Fixed in that reign of cold? While here
Fevers eat the flesh away
Leaving a torment at the bone.

Now from the cobbles of the town
In the blank hours before the light,
Winds gather up the dust and blow
Its grains about your feet of stone;

Your voice breaks on my driven sleep,
I fling my arms out in the dark:
Empty; your voice trails in my own
Its cry I stifled long ago.

FILM-CLIPS

1. TRANSLATION FROM A FILM BY BERGMAN

for Margaret Walters

His sleeping heartbeat tolls him out to walk
The strange familiar city. There all windows
Have become blind. It is not night nor day,
He is awake and sleeping: wherever he turns,
Colour bleached out of them, the streets are empty
But for the dust driven by absent wind.
Sound is deaf, time is not here, the hands
Are gone from every clockface: life has stopped
But has not ceased. Called by his fearful blood,
He treads on, and treads.
                   On a null pavement
Suddenly a standing figure
Turns, bringing his own dead crumpled face.

2. OPENING SEQUENCE

for William Fitzwater

A girl is standing on hills above the sea
In clear grey light: waves below break gently
On rounded stones, a wind stirs grass and hair;
She draws her cloak about her as the land
Draws to itself the grey folds of the sea.

Waiting: and for a thing not yet revealed,
But prophesied by the wind, by footsteps sounding
In the passages of the blood. Nerves quicken and cry;
She turns about, and turns once more, full circle:
On land and sea, nothing; yet the event
Is imminent, it is running through the skin
As a gust in the leaves of a tree. Now she is staring
At the dawn sea, her body intent and still,
Only her clothes and her hair living.
Behind her without sound
A figure has come: a note strikes in her frame:
Terror and expectation: she turns to face him.

MOTHER AND DAUGHTER

Her gold eyes drink the light. She is a woman
I see: although my child.
Along the avenue of nerves a wind
Stings my dead leaves to hissing.
Her face has no more beauty than my own,
But her body: there, the knives of vision tell me,
She speaks a language someone
Will pay high fees to learn. As I must learn
To love once more through hatred.

JUDAS ISCARIOT

Judas mercator . . . denariorum
numero Christum Judaeis
tradidit.
— *Matins of Maundy Thursday*

Why not, when pity stirs, lament the damned?
Conceived in the anonymous dark,
Nurtured and borne through pain to the bright earth,
Suckled at the world's breast: to be at length
Offered the wind, the bread and wine, the word.
Surely the man can call our flesh to mourning
Who traded these away for a few pence,
Then saw the whole plan monstrous and inane,
And with a howl
As the cock stretched its throat and crew
Went to his tree upon the precipice.

ANNA BRENNAN'S HOUSE

for my Mother

The roof of slate is drawn down in the moonlight,
Windows catch a glow not from within,
The grass is high, weeds are among the roses
And over the steps, creepers and trees draw close,
All gathering on the house as though intent
To muffle sound, to heap a growing silence.
Garden and house are grey under the moon,
A scatter of flowers cresting the grass with white,
And a white cap of blossom on a pear-tree
Leaning towards a pane that cannot see.

She who lived here is dead, all these remind me.
The vigour of her mind, the warmth and wit,
My mother still recalls like her own youth.
Now all she was, all she became, is gone;
But this calm place lays on the arm a wrinkled
And gracious hand: No grief. What is it here,
In these unspeaking things her life has touched,
That so persuades me of her present heaven?
I pause these moments on the weed-grown path
And for her sake offer my quiet breathing.

Kew, October 1962

THE MOON AT DAWN

SONG FOR GUITAR OR LUTE

She came into my room
After the moon was down;
With a young girl's daring
Came beside my bed:
'Rise up, love,' she said,
'I have come: take me.'
It was no dream, but I
Lay in the sleep of fear.
She called with insistent pleading;
Called; turned at last away.
Now, worn, unrested
I wake to the hollow day.

LAMENT AND PRAYER

after the Dutch

You my sun,
Who brought spring to my hills:
Since you withdraw from me,
Nearer and warm
Shine on another soon.
You gather clouds about you,
The spring day's at an end,
Over my pleasure-pools
That lie swept of your light
The chill breezes run.
Love you must rise elsewhere
(And I, turn and descend
Once more towards night):
O make it summer there.

AFTERTASTE

So, love, you must go hungry again: not even
The half loaf I could offer,
The dangerous foreign bread. Perhaps you will say,
'Yes: yes I did rightly',
Pacing the room with fingertips together,
Bird-glanced, taut with freedom;
Even to yourself acknowledge no regrets;
Call in your friends, be gay
With coffee or a sip of sherry. And dwell
In secret on another,
Who offered nothing and is safe to yearn for.

THE TEMPTATION OF SAINT ANTHONY

Famished, and God still wanting, yet with zeal
To rouse desire for Him in hearts asleep
In their own fullness: now, when heat is a burden
On the dry reeds and slows the crickets' pulse,
He makes his way to the city, that great desert.

By some ignored, by some taken in kindly.
God is not mocked, nor he. But the great buildings,
The streets and gardens where the plane leaves spread
Their intercession between man and sun,
The brown and golden flesh everywhere bending
To flesh, other and the same, as naturally
As heads of grain in a summer field of breeze:
These will not hear of fasting or denial,
Or word of worlds beyond. God before clay?
God within clay they cleave to. None are tempted,
Neither they nor he. They have already
The words of life, its leisured flow, and he,
Intent on a far cry, is a watercourse
Which for a season the river has forgotten:
The cream-brown flesh of a particular woman,
Her sure, gracious, offering glance towards him,
He sees with calm blood still, and passes on.

Again to the waste. But now it is thronged: from youth
The soft shapes on a stone pillow lean
Lost substance, forever never to touch,
Eyes from which his own once swerved away

And hands not taken; married perhaps with dust.
The long thorn again and again runs in;
There is no God, although he calls, beyond
A voice in the hot reeds: Be still and know
That this temptation is sufficient for you.
At the quick of night, beside his caverned bed,
She lies on summer grass where the dew gathers,
A girl long in oblivion: as in a game
She wears a monk's brown habit; her dark hair short,
But her face a woman's: in the sleep of sense
Waiting intent, and her still lips reproaching:
How easily once you could have reached and held me.

To the city, back in flight: to a love of flesh
Offered and found. Late, late,
But found. From that embrace not to return.

Paris: Amsterdam

June 1967

DIALOGUE

No God, none, she said. And he said: Love
Is God. I pray, when I come in at your gates
You catch at the saint's experience: all an outflowing,
A flowing-together, confounding of words. She
Drew him in closer. His voice, quick, ran on;
Here was the resurrection, in their flesh,
God's very breath. Dear love, to me, she said,
All this means nothing. Thrust in against me, hard.

A RING

In love still by unsinging light I labour
To persuade words together,
Gauche girls at a ballet lesson,
Wayward, shy of the teaching mirror:

And you remain unpraised;
No man has taken you and not passed on.
You hang your dark head still: still I remember
How once your breast welcomed a freezing hand.

Since nothing stays for you
In life, I would at least
Get words to spin into a frozen shape,
A ring for your chilled finger
From my still colder hand.

STILL

They, many my friends,
Are fleet to plunge into the surf which greets them;
Glide with strong ease down wind to a sure nest;
Store patient honey until it overflows.

But you, and you, and I
Are held; dammed, with no flood;
Are like the stamping horses on a shield
That prance, hooves reared, a mockery of motion
Still as their flat ground. Are figures on a screen
Frozen just at the moment where our lips
Open to speak, our hands
Reach out to the cheek's curve the fruited bough.

THE MOON AT DAWN

Between two loves. The stillness at night's end:
Dumb streets, no cars, no walkers;
From houses, life withdrawn;

The roof of cloud beginning to break up
For a sky soaked with light:
The east, and a moon that swiftly
Drops through shelving clouds, like a prized coin
Cast by rite to the regardless sea.

The moon at dawn: the two lights for once
Flooding the sky together, before one sinks
And the dark sight where life is in abeyance
Turns eastward with a faint joy, half mistrustful.

MUSIC IN SUMMER

Love, you were foretold me,
Though it was not in words
Nor a girl's waking flesh nor the quick of her breathing,

Long before yours were gathered,
Even before the seed
First welled and strangely flooded through my night:

I was a child still,
Hearing music in summer
Breathe with a life beyond it. When I passed

Then through the tall doors
Open to the summer night—
Warm air, leaves among light, the receptive city—

Unguessed but certain, your young hands had touched me.

THE SEAL

When for the first time I kissed you
Under the new leaves when the dew was heavy,
You kissed me back as a tide begins to flow
Strongly between the narrows.
You leaned into the left side of my mouth;
Said in that gesture,
Heedless, eloquent as a sleeper's posture,
'This is my seal, by this
Know it is I who kiss.'

LOVE POEMS FROM A SEQUENCE

I

In what dark room soever we lie down,
Let there be darkness for the eyes only,
And keep outside its walls
Whatever fear can choke the cry in the throat,
And halt the deeper current.
In what dark room soever, when we lie down
Pray to hear battle at your gates, the drums
The flutes of victory in the narrow pass.

II

We must give thought to circles, yet be selective,
Avoid the whirlpool turning in the mind,
Dismal and slow, sucking the small boat down.
Best to go inland: still within sound of the sea
Choose some green clearing for our dancing ring,
Each of us draw a circle round the other
And dance the other in.

EMBLEM

EMBLEM

for Alec King

Where at Nicæa the palace of Constantine
Once stood, and now a bare tree spreads its branches
Over a few stones by violet water,

A grader lately pushing earth aside
Sank to a vaulted tomb. Sunlight discovered
Grief outweighed: paintings on every wall

Still fresh in greens and reds and ripe wheat colour.
On the far wall two peacocks,
Emblems of immortality, between them

An urn brimming green the waters of heaven,
And on the floor below, a heap of bones
Blent by pyre and time to the wall's yellow.

One composition: the mortal shards resigned,
The long necked peacocks, tails furled, at their urn
Sipping forever.

Book designed by David Walker
Set and printed at The
Griffin Press, Adelaide,
South Australia